The Black-Footed Ferret

Written and Illustrated by J. M. Roever

Steck-Vaughn Company

An Intext Publisher

Austin, Texas

Library of Congress Cataloging in Publication Data
Roever, J   M
   The black-footed ferret.
   SUMMARY: Describes the habits and behavior of an en-
dangered species of American wildlife, the black-footed ferret,
a member of the weasel family.
   1. Black-footed ferret—Juvenile literature. 2. Rare ani-
mals—Juvenile literature. [1. Black-footed ferret. 2. Weasels.
3. Rare animals]
I. Title.
PZ10.R617BI   599'.74447   72-542
ISBN 0-8114-7749-5

The Black-Footed Ferret

A streak of light fur sparkles in the moonlight. Suddenly, the black shoebutton eyes, black-masked face, black-stockinged feet, and black-tipped tail disappear into the darkness. This pale phantom of the prairie is one of North America's rarest mammals—the black-footed ferret.

So uncommon and secretive is the black-footed ferret that it remained unnamed and unrecorded until little more than 120 years ago. Then in 1851 the famous artist and naturalist John J. Audubon and his friend, John Bachman, identified and named the unusual little animal.

If a black-footed ferret wore an identification tag, it would look like this:

Class—Mammal (They nurse their young.)
Order—Carnivora (kar-<u>niv</u>-uh-ruh), "Meat Eater"
Scientific Family Name—Mustelidae (mus-<u>tel</u>-uh-dee), "Musk Carriers"
Genus: Scientific Describing Name—Mustela nigripes (mus-<u>tee</u>-luh <u>nye</u>-grih-pays), "Black-Footed Musk Carrier"
Common Name—Black-Footed Ferret

The Sioux Indians called
the black-footed ferret
"black-faced prairie dog."
Many superstitions of the
Plains Indians revolved
around this strange little
animal. Its pelt was often
used as a sacred object
in tribal ceremonies.

**Headdress of Indian Chief
Using Black-Footed
Ferret Skins
(Cheyenne and Blackfeet)**

**Pass your hand in front
of your eyes to represent
a mask.**

Make a Z with your arm.

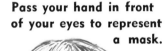

Point to something black.

**Plains Indian Sign Language
for Black-Footed Ferret**

3

Where Black-Footed Ferrets Live

The black-footed ferret is a creature of the short-grass prairie. Never abundant, it is rare throughout all of its range. Today most reports of existing ferrets come from South Dakota.

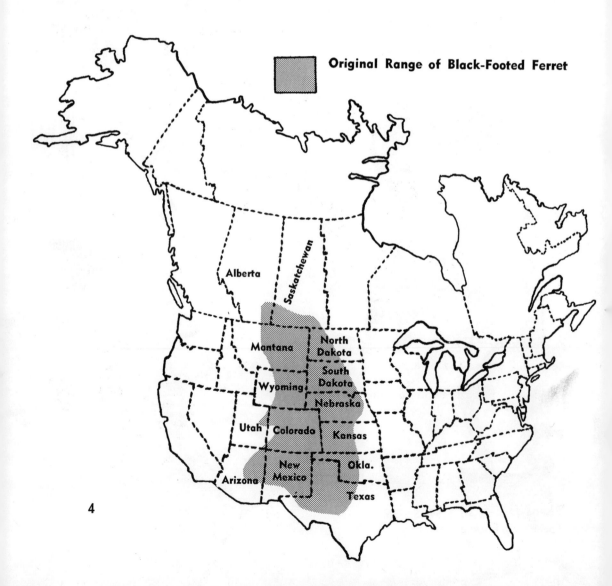

Original Range of Black-Footed Ferret

Mustelidae—The Musk Carriers

The black-footed ferret is the largest North American weasel. Ferrets and their relatives have scent or musk glands beneath their tails. Skunks possess greatly developed musk glands which spray strong, unpleasant scent. The glands of the black-footed ferret are poorly developed, and their odor is less noticeable.

River Otter

Marten

Mink

Wolverine

Fisher

Black-Footed Ferret

Spotted Skunk

Badger

Long-Tailed Weasel

5

Occasionally, fitch ferrets, imported for hunting, scientific experiments, or pets, are mistaken for black-footed ferrets. Notice the diference between the two animals.

Rough Fur

Small Ears

Light Mask

Tapered Tail

Pointed Muzzle

Round Body

⅔ Tail Tip Black

European Fitch Ferret

Ferreting—A Way To Hunt

The fitch ferret is an Old World cousin of the black-footed ferret. In many countries of Europe, ferreting is a popular way to hunt. A tame fitch ferret is released at the entrance of a wild rabbit's den. The ferret locates and pursues the rabbit underground. To escape the ferret, the rabbit dashes from its burrow and is caught in the hunter's net.

A ferret searches for rabbits in burrows.

6

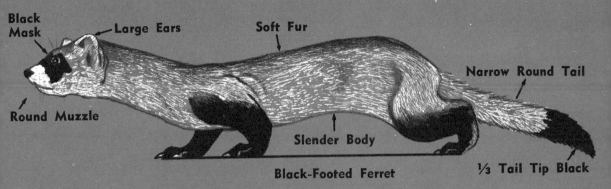

Black Mask

Large Ears

Soft Fur

Narrow Round Tail

Round Muzzle

Slender Body

⅓ Tail Tip Black

Black-Footed Ferret

Have You Ever Gone Ferreting?

The word ferret actually means "little thief." It comes from the Latin word fur—meaning "thief." If you look up "ferret" in the dictionary, you will learn that it is also a verb. It means "to search for with great care and constant effort."

You ferret for answers in books.

Appearance and Senses of Ferrets

The cautious black-footed ferret is mainly a nocturnal (nok-<u>ter</u>-nul), or night-roaming animal. Its eyes glow bright green in the reflection of man-made lights. Excellent eyesight enables the ferret to travel about on moonless nights and in dark, underground burrows. This animal's sensitive nose constantly tests the air for telltale odors of food or danger, and its large, round ears catch every airborne sound. The ferret's front paws and long, sturdy claws are well equipped for digging.

Soft, beige-colored fur provides the ferret with camouflage (<u>kam</u>-uh-flahzh) by blending with the colors of soil and dry grass. Most weasels shed their summer coats for furs of winter white. The fur of the black-footed ferret remains the same color but grows slightly longer in winter.

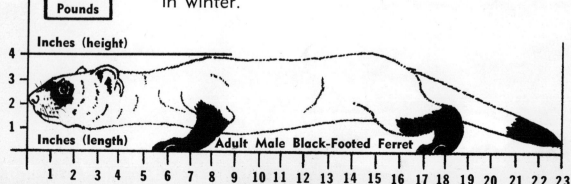

2 ¼ Pounds

Inches (height)

4
3
2
1

Inches (length) Adult Male Black-Footed Ferret

1 2 3 4 5 6 7 8 9 10 11 12 13 14 15 16 17 18 19 20 21 22 23

The Black-Footed Ferret

The Voice of the Ferret

Usually quiet and secretive, the black-footed ferret has many ways of voicing its displeasure. Like an angry house cat, it spits and hisses boldly. An alarmed ferret chatters and barks.

A protective mother ferret calls her young with soft, begging grunts.

Enemies of the Ferret

Badgers, coyotes, hawks, owls, eagles, and large snakes are natural enemies of the ferret. Dogs, cats, guns, traps, cars, and poison also take their toll of this rare mammal. Ticks, mites, and fleas often bother the black-footed ferret, while diseases such as distemper or pneumonia (nyoo-moh-nee-uh) may cause the ferret's death.

11

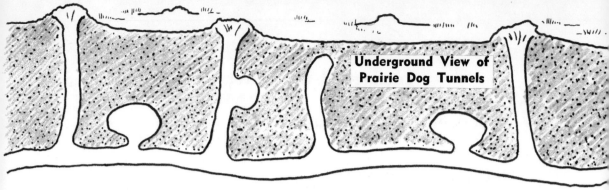

Underground View of Prairie Dog Tunnels

The Prairie Dog

It would be impossible to learn about the black-footed ferret without meeting another animal of the grassy plains—the prairie dog. One of the most unusual associations in nature exists between these two animals. The prairie dog, unwillingly, supplies the ferret with meals and shelter. The ferret occasionally finds other food, but its preference is a plump prairie pup.

The prairie dog is a type of ground squirrel. Its yapping voice earned it the title of "dog." Prairie dogs dwell in underground burrows. All the burrows in one area are called a prairie dog town.

When danger threatens, the prairie dogs dive into their burrows. In underground tunnels, prairie dogs can escape from coyotes, hawks, and bobcats—but not from black-footed ferrets.

What the Black-Footed Ferret Eats

Prairie Dog

Insect

Mouse

Cottontail Rabbit

Birds' Eggs

Ground Squirrel

Bird

Rat

Reptile

13

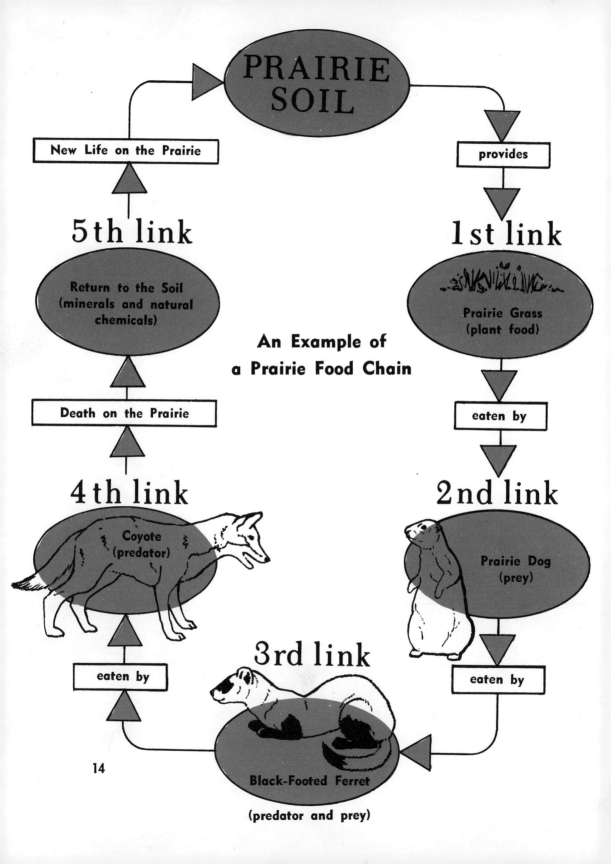

PRAIRIE SOIL

New Life on the Prairie

5th link

Return to the Soil (minerals and natural chemicals)

Death on the Prairie

4th link

Coyote (predator)

eaten by

3rd link

Black-Footed Ferret

(predator and prey)

provides

1st link

Prairie Grass (plant food)

eaten by

2nd link

Prairie Dog (prey)

eaten by

An Example of a Prairie Food Chain

14

Predator and Prey—Links in a Food Chain

Almost all animals can be identified as either predators or prey, or both. Predators are meat eaters that devour other creatures. Animals which are eaten are known as prey. Every animal is part of a marvelous food chain that keeps the world of nature in balance. The first link in the chain shown on page 14 is plant food provided by the prairie soil.

Prairie dogs are the second link in this chain, because they eat the prairie grass and are the prey of the black-footed ferret. If the predator-ferret is eaten by another predator, such as a coyote, the ferret becomes prey and the third food link.

When the coyote dies, its body breaks down to become a part of the prairie soil. New grass grows up and provides nourishment for more prairie animals. The fourth and fifth links in nature's chain of food and life are completed.

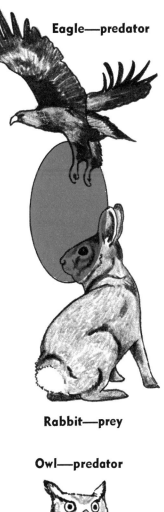

Eagle—predator

Rabbit—prey

Owl—predator

Mouse—prey

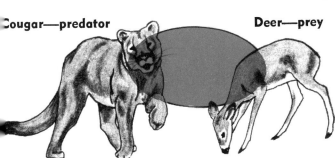

Cougar—predator   Deer—prey

15

The Plight of the Prairie Dog

Because of its relationship with the prairie dog, the black-footed ferret is almost always found in a prairie dog town. Abandoned burrows provide ready-made housing for the ferret. The dens are cool in summer, warm in winter. A puddle of water in the basement tunnel supplies a place to drink. With a bit of digging, the ferret remodels the den and sets up housekeeping in the midst of its favorite food supply.

The unfortunate prairie dogs do not accept their new neighbor without some resistance. As soon as the ferret enters a burrow, prairie dogs rush forward and attempt to fill up the hole with dirt. They dig and shove soil down into the den. But the ferret soon pokes its way back out.

16

Prairie Dogs

Left Front Foot

Left Hind Foot

The black-footed ferret usually hunts at night while prairie dogs are sleeping. Before retiring, prairie dogs reinforce their burrows against a visit from an unwelcome intruder. They block the entrance to their den with soil from the inside of the tunnel. But the black-masked "little thief" has no difficulty unlocking the doorway to the prairie dog's home.

The Trench Maker

When the ferret digs for its dinner or removes soil from its own den, it creates a trench of excavated soil. Each time it backs out of the prairie dog's burrow, the ferret holds a load of loosened dirt against its chest. With every trip, the ferret hauls its burden farther from the burrow and piles soil in a neat line above the ground. After many journeys back and forth, a narrow trench—perhaps as long as 9 feet—is formed.

19

Trenches at a prairie dog town indicate the activity of ferrets.

The drama of life and death between prairie dog and black-footed ferret occurs far beneath the earth in the darkness of night. There the narrow tunnels of the burrow block the prairie dog's chances to defend itself. The hungry ferret quickly overpowers his prey, and in a few seconds the deed is done.

During the day the black-footed ferret
finds the prairie dog difficult to capture
above the ground. If seized by a ferret,
the prairie dog often rolls on its back
and defends itself with teeth and claws.

Two or three prairie dogs may join
forces and attempt to attack the ferret.
Sometimes a prairie dog chases the ferret,
while at other times the ferret chases a
prairie dog. Usually the ferret retreats
to its burrow, as if to lure the prairie
dog inside.

A Puzzling Question

The black-footed ferret has an important purpose in nature's balance of life on the prairie—to prey upon and help control prairie dog populations. There would not be enough plant food for all prairie dogs if too many of them remained in one area.

Due to its secretive behavior, the black-footed ferret has always been difficult to study in the wild. Biologists wonder what force in nature has controlled ferret populations so that they never become abundant predators.

Family Life

Adult ferrets travel alone throughout fall and winter. By April or May they seek mates, and about six weeks later the birth of 4 to 6 baby ferrets takes place in a remodeled prairie-dog burrow. The early life of a ferret is one of nature's well-guarded secrets. The mother ferret cares for her young alone and nurses them until they are old enough to eat meat. By July the young ferrets cautiously appear at the entrance to the burrow.

Mother ferret shifts her family to a new burrow many times during the summer. The moves provide unsoiled shelters for her growing young and allow her to hunt closer to prairie dog tunnels containing fresh prey.

Young ferrets are very shy and timid. The mother ferret must often pull them out of the burrow by the nape of the neck. As they grow bolder, the little ferrets run with bouncing leaps and play like puppies at the opening of their den.

When they follow their mother in single file, the ferret family resembles a child's pull toy.

Sometimes the female ferret drags a dead prairie dog to her family's den, or she may lead her young to another burrow where a meal is hidden.

By late summer or early fall the ferrets have learned to hunt for themselves. As winter nears, the ferret family separates. Each of the adult-size young sets out to look for its own prairie dog hunting ground.

Buffalo

Pronghorn

Deer

Elk

Wild Horse

Prairie Dog

Poison on the Prairie

Before the American West was settled, prairie grass provided food for buffalo, pronghorns, wild horses, deer, elk, prairie dogs, and many other wild animals. Today the western grasslands are used for grazing sheep and cattle. Wild animals that eat grass or kill livestock are not wanted on the range.

The United States government controls unwanted wildlife with poison. A deadly chemical called Compound 1080 has been used to poison coyotes, wolves, bobcats, and other predatory animals and birds.

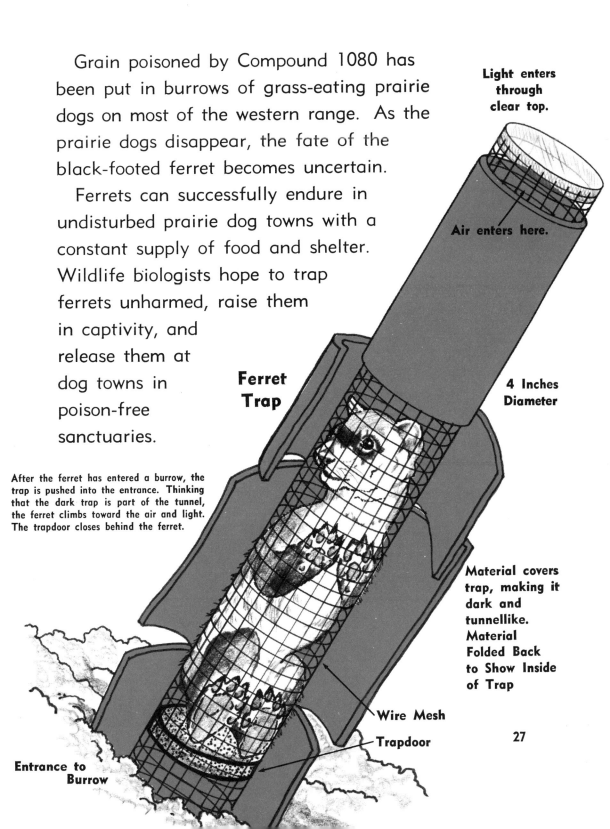

Grain poisoned by Compound 1080 has been put in burrows of grass-eating prairie dogs on most of the western range. As the prairie dogs disappear, the fate of the black-footed ferret becomes uncertain.

Ferrets can successfully endure in undisturbed prairie dog towns with a constant supply of food and shelter. Wildlife biologists hope to trap ferrets unharmed, raise them in captivity, and release them at dog towns in poison-free sanctuaries.

After the ferret has entered a burrow, the trap is pushed into the entrance. Thinking that the dark trap is part of the tunnel, the ferret climbs toward the air and light. The trapdoor closes behind the ferret.

Light enters through clear top.

Air enters here.

Ferret Trap

4 Inches Diameter

Material covers trap, making it dark and tunnellike. Material Folded Back to Show Inside of Trap

Wire Mesh

Trapdoor

Entrance to Burrow

27

Steller's Sea Cow

Will the Black-Footed Ferret Survive?

Sea Mink

Eastern Elk

In your lifetime the fate of the black-footed ferret will be decided. It may pass tragically into extinction with the eastern elk, the sea mink, the Steller's sea cow, and others. Perhaps concerned Americans will find a way to preserve our endangered wildlife. Then the black-footed ferret, pale phantom of the prairie, will peer through black goggles at a world that promises an environment in which all creatures can survive.

Bald Eagle

Brown Pelican

These Endangered Animals Belong to you!

Their Future Is in your Care!

Black-Footed Ferret

Red Wolf

Swift or Kit Fox

Bluebird at
Handmade
Nesting Box

What Can You Do To Protect Wildlife?

All the wild animals in our country belong to a very special person—YOU! When someone imperils a ferret, shoots an eagle, traps a wild horse, poisons a coyote, destroys a marsh, or pollutes a river, he is harming wildlife belonging to you.

All wild creatures are owned by each United States citizen. You can help to PRESERVE your wildlife if you follow these guides:

Protect—wildlife on your property.

Read—wildlife books and magazines.

Educate—yourself about wildlife.

Send—letters to Congressmen for help.

Educate—others about imperiled wildlife.

Respect—laws protecting wildlife.

Volunteer—helping hands for wildlife.

Enroll—in conservation groups.